AZ91E AS CASTINGS

ANIL KUMAR MATTA

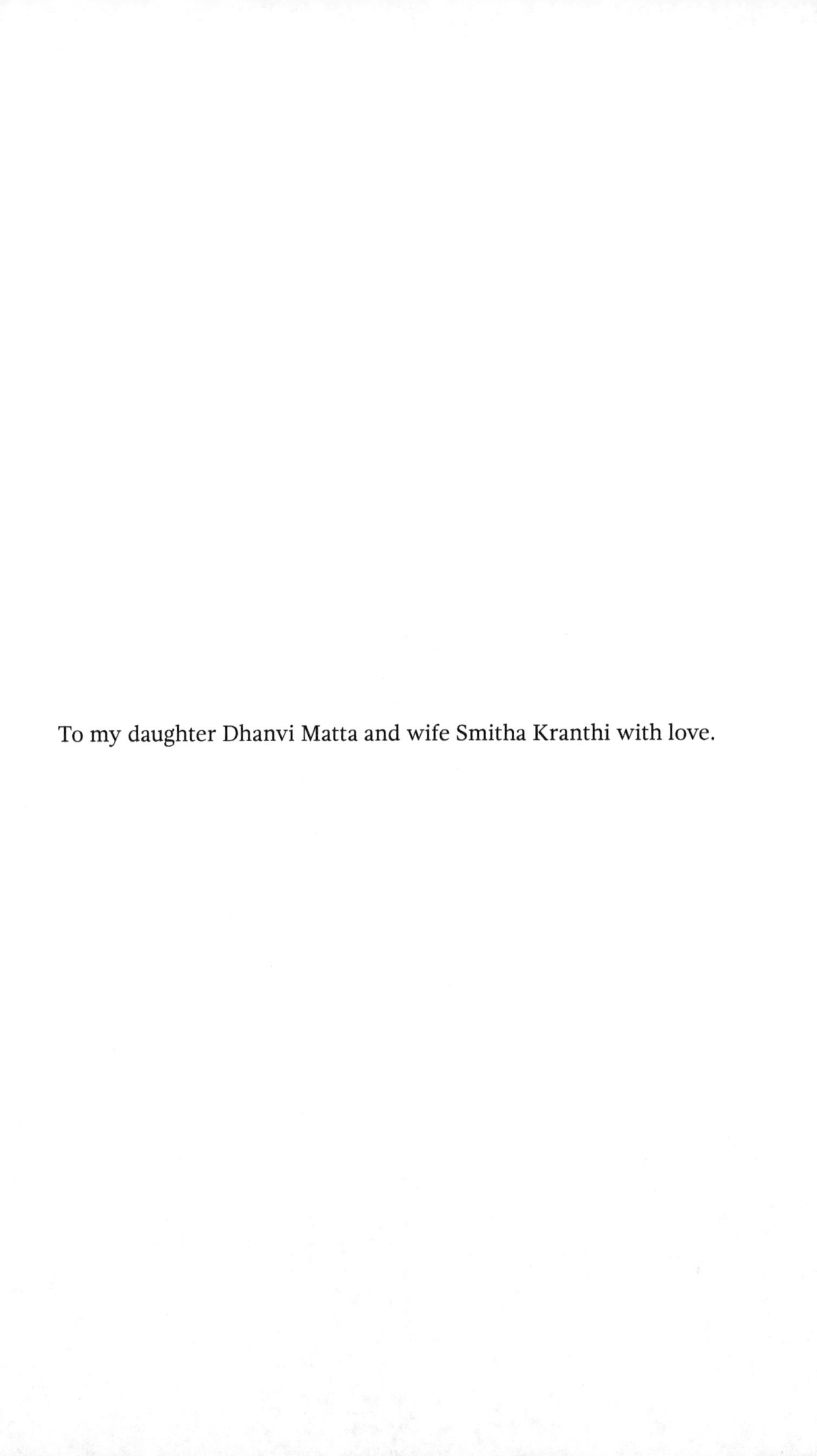

To my daughter Dhanvi Matta and wife Smitha Kranthi with love.

Contents

Foreword

This work helps all research Scholars & Engineering aspirants to select Magnesium alloy problem and solve it by ease. As such applications of all *AZ Series Magnesium alloys* to real world are shown.

We are unable to use AZ Series for bike side luggage box where it has robust space.

We are unable to use AZ Series as helmet holder (front end above fuel tank) while travelling.

We are unable to use AZ Series as spark plugs where vehicle stops frequently and never starts in winter and rainy days.

We are unable to use AZ Series for lighter weights chassis for bikes and cars.

Even we are unable to use AZ Series to reduce the weight of full helmet completely.

We are unable to use AZ Series for Highway light way post, open air theater posts, high way banner posts.

As mentioned in my previous books, due to cost AZ Series is completely out of the reach to human kind.

Also we were unable to control the high heat from exhaust pipes.

This work helps the researcher to select a problem and uplift human kind.

Anil Kumar Matta
CEO- Natas Consultancy

Preface

This book gives vast sight about society based applications of AZ series and a clear cut picture of materials, where one can use them for several purposes. Removing Prons and Corns generating the branch, helps a researcher to attain his/her goal.

Natas consultancy, Vijayawada, developed many automobile parts especially tractor rockshaft arm, four wheeler accelerator pedal, brake rotor. This huge research helps the reader to understand and utilize the alloys in applying for real world problem.

Anil Kumar Matta

CEO- Natas Consultancy

Acknowledgements

First of all, I thank Christ for showing mercy on me in all my endeavour of my life.

Next, I thank my beloved wife A SMITHA KRANTHI and daughter MATTA DHANVI for their continuous support in holding me to take this work forward without which it is impossible to construct a work or a book. Their support especially when I cracked as job as Advisor and as Associate Professor in Mechanical Engineering Department, GVR & S Engineering College, Budampadu, Guntur, AP, India, without which it is highly impossible with only two hands. I also thank my Aunt A SRI RANI, A STEPHY DOLLY, BANNU, CHINNU, CHITTI AUNTY for traveling with my life.

I thank from my deepest heart to my parents MATTA KISHORE KUMAR and SARADA DEVI in holding my hand in this deepest journey. Severe heights and downs never affected me because of my beloved parents.

I thank my brothers MATTA SUNIL KUMAR and MATTA KIRAN KUMAR (Late) in travelling to deepest darkness in time of hard and tough days.

I thank four children MATTA DHANVI, MATTA SHRUTI, MATTA MANSI, MATTA SHERWIN and their MOMS in laughing with me at happiest days of my life.

Finally I take pride in devoting the present work to my consultancy and newly portioned state AP. Lastly I thank all my relatives, friends, students who have travelled in all the endeavour of my life. It's unforgettable to have mother earth to give places like Rajam, Bobbili, Vizag, Vijayawada (MOMS PLACE), Tenali (AUNTS PLACE), Paritala, Budampadu, Guntur.

Thanks to all for this memorable life.

Anil Kumar Matta

CEO- Natas Consultancy

Ph: (+91) 9652842089/ 8096558651

Email: anilkumarmatta7@gmail.com

Website: https://rapid-prototyping-consultancy.business.site

Prologue

The Ministry of Mines is responsible for managing the Mines and Minerals Act of 1957 with regard to all mines and minerals other than coal, usual gas, and petroleum as well as for surveying and investigating all minerals, excluding common gases, petroleum, and atomic minerals, as well as for mining and metallurgy of non-ferrous materials like aluminium, copper, zinc, sn, gold, and nickel, among others.

CHAPTER ONE

OLD STONE, MEDIEVAL AND MODERN AGES

To categorise major eras in the history of the world, time periods are grouped into the following three categories:

Early History

Ancient History

Recent History

The earliest known human settlements were discovered approximately 6000 BC, during ancient history. Around 650 AD, several significant empires, including the Roman Empire, the Han Empire of China, and the Gupta Empire, come to an end.

Post-classical history, commonly referred to as mediaeval history, is thought to have started approximately 500 AD, following the significant cultural and theological upheaval that was typical at this time.

The Modern Period includes all extracontinental expansions from the time of the Europeans' exploration and colonisation of Asia and North America until the present.Aluminum, zinc, manganese, silicon, copper, rare earth elements, and zirconium are frequently used in the production of magnesium alloys, which are combinations of magnesium (the lightest structural metal) and other metals.

CHAPTER TWO

MAGNESIUM ALLOYS

The lightest structural alloys are known to be those made of magnesium. Magnesium, the thinnest structural metal, is combined with other metal components to give them better physical characteristics. Manganese, aluminium, zinc, silicon, copper, zirconium, and rare-earth metals are a few of these elements.

Magnesium has some advantageous characteristics, such as a low specific gravity and a high strength-to-weight ratio. Because of this, the material is well suited for use in a variety of commercial, industrial, electrical, biomedical, and automotive applications.

The several types of magnesium alloys and their names, the physical characteristics of magnesium alloys, and the purposes for which they are used are all explained here.

Cast alloys and wrought alloys are the two main categories of magnesium alloys.

Cast alloys are often created by pouring molten metal into a mould, where it cools and takes on the desired shape. Magnesium is commonly found in cast alloys, and its main alloying elements include aluminium, manganese, and zinc, all in varying proportions (although never more than 10%). Zirconium and rare-earth metals have both lately been employed as alloying elements, primarily to improve creep resistance. Heat treatments also improve the mechanical characteristics of cast alloys.

Contrarily, wrought alloys are alloys that are mechanically worked to get the required shape by processes including forging, extrusion, and rolling. The main alloying components are also aluminium, manganese, and zinc. alloys for wrought.

Applications for structural materials can be found in the automotive, aerospace, industrial, and commercial sectors. Because of their light weight, high strength-to-weight, high stiffness-to-weight, castability, machinability, and excellent damping, magnesium alloys are a good choice for these applications.

CHAPTER THREE

RELEVANCE OF MG ALLOYS

Alloy for magnesium: AZ91E-T6

Designates the two primary alloying elements in the first component (AZ) (aluminium, zinc)

Determines the percentage amount of the primary alloying elements in the second portion (91). (9 percent and 1 percent , respectively)

Differentiates alloys with the same amounts of the primary alloying elements in the third portion (E) (fifth standardised alloy with the above percentages)

The fourth section (T6) indicates the alloy's state (temper)

Magnesium alloys are sought-after materials primarily because of their excellent machinability, high strength-to-weight ratios, and inexpensive cost. Compared to other common alloys like aluminium or steel alloys, they have a low specific gravity of 1.74 g/cm3 and a comparatively low Young's modulus (42 GPa). However, at room temperature, they are fragile and poorly formable. They become more moldable as the temperature rises, but it takes a lot of energy. Additionally, research has shown that by weakening the Mg alloys' basic texture, formability can be improved at the expense of strength.

The third most popular non-ferrous casting material is magnesium alloys. Based on their chemical compositions, the alloys' physical characteristics vary. Different alloying elements would produce different qualities under certain circumstances.

Aluminum enhances the alloy's strength, hardness, and ductility, which makes the casting process easier.

Strength at room temperature, casting fluidity, and corrosion resistance are all improved by zinc.

By generating intermetallic compounds with metals that resemble iron and removing them after melting, manganese boosts the resilience of AM and AZ alloys against seawater corrosion.

Rare earth metals work to strengthen materials, reduce porosity and weld cracking, and resist high-temperature creep and corrosion.

When added to zinc and rare earth metal alloys, zirconium is a potent grain refiner.

During casting and welding, beryllium aids in reducing surface oxidation.

Calcium improves grain refining, which aids in managing the alloy's metallurgy.

1. Relevance of AZ Series: AZ91E

Electronic applications include hard drive arms, mobile phone and portable media device housings, as well as electronic packaging. Due to their light weight, strength, and durability, magnesium alloys are utilised in place of plastics. Additionally, they offer comparatively greater heat dissipation and electromagnetic and radio frequency interference protection.

Magnesium alloys are ideal for wheelchairs and portable medical equipment that require lightweight materials. Due to magnesium's biocompatibility and bioabsorbability, cardiovascular stents and orthopaedic devices are further possible applications of some magnesium alloys.

Automotive: housing for the transmission, clutch and brake support brackets aircraft landing gear, rotor fittings, and gearbox housings Industrial: machinery that operates quickly, as textile machines. Commercial items include ladders, hand tools, and luggage.

A high speed train is a type of vehicle that can travel at a high speed continuously; its top speed is often greater than 200 km/h. Modern highspeed vehicles include highspeed trains, which embody the best science and technology available for trains. Highspeed trains may significantly increase train travel speed and increase the effectiveness of rail transportation.

Many nations throughout the world firmly support the use of new highspeed trains to fulfil the rising demand for travel since they are quick, comfortable, stable, safe, energy-saving, and ecologically beneficial.

Since the opening of the world's first highspeed train in Japan on October 1, 1964, with a top speed of approximately 440 kilometres, many other nations have started to develop highspeed railways, and train speeds have continued to increase.

item	magnesium	aluminum
atomic weight	12	13
density 20g/cm3	1.74	2.7
melting point	650	660
specific heat KJ/m3	1.03	0.9
latent heat of melting KJ/kg	368	397
coefficient of heat conductivity W/M.K	154	220
coefficient of thermal expansion×10-6	25.2	23.6

Mg-alloys	AZ31B	H112	160-200	280-320	94	95-97	92	14-21
	AZ80	T5	267	350		72		
	ZK60	T6	305-350	365-410			94	11-15
	Mg-Zn-Y-Zr	T6	321	356			93	7
	AZ91	O	280	331		80		12
	5083	H111	125-200	275-350		90	93	12-15
	5083	0	148	298			100	23.0
	5083	H321	153	305			91	22.5
	6005A	T6	200-225	250-270	75			6-8
	6061	T6	270	290	75	64	84	12
Al -alloys	6082	T6	250-260	290-310	78	67	83	8-10
	6082	T4	149	260			93	18.8
	7005	T6	270-290	340-350		71		8
	7N01	T5	290	345	84		82	
	7018	T79	245	350			95	11
	7020	T6	348	395	77		78	12

High Speed Train AZ91E Properties

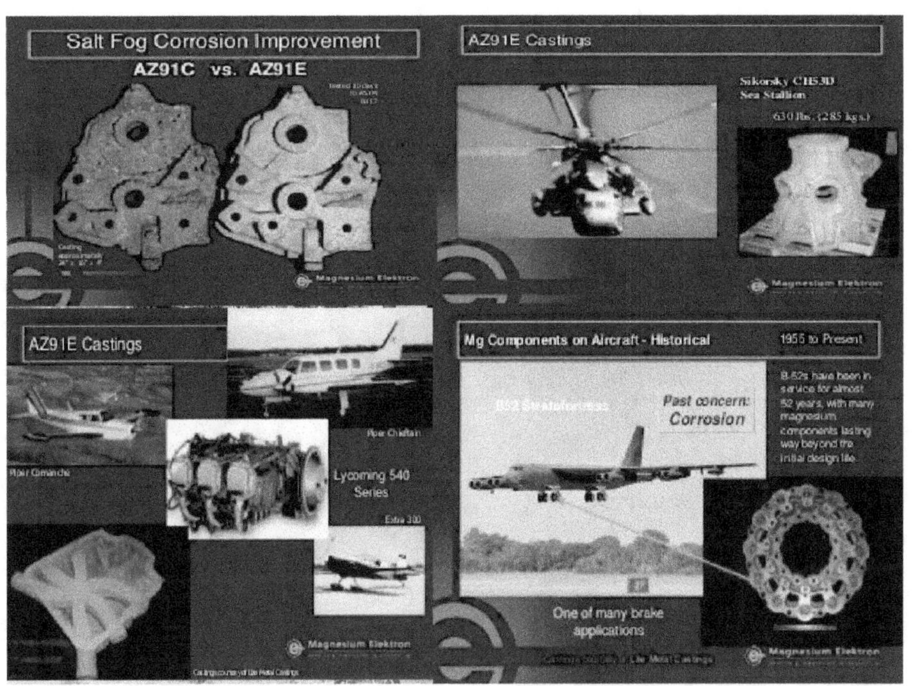

AZ91E Casting Pictures

OUTCOMES AND PONDERINGS

- AZ91E is used for Casting in Trains, Hellicophters and Aircrafts.
- AZ91E can allevate the strengths of Cast Irons in Casting form.

REFERENCES

1. A.K.Matta. AZ91E towards GCI: Notion Press, ISBN: 9798887332239, 2022.

2. A.K.Matta. Examination of AZ91E with Ni0.21 Ca0.03: Notion Press, ISBN: 9798887176918, 2022.

3. A.K.Matta. Making of AZ91E Series: Notion Press, ISBN: 9798887176369, 2022.

4. A.K.Matta. MATLAB to Scallable Learning: Notion Press, ISBN: 9798887176635, 2022.

5. A.K.Matta. Allaying of Tractor Wing: More Books, ISBN: 9786138959502, 2021.

6. Modified R.S.Arm. Patent. 201641034578,2021.

7. Anil Kumar Matta., Recent Studies on particle reinforcement AZ91 Magnesium Composites Fabricated by Stir Casting- A Review , JMEE 2020 , pp 115-126, ISBN:2544-0780.

8. A.K.Matta., Metallic Product Prototyping, testing and web visibility for manufacturers. Reference module in materials science and materials Engineering, Oxford: Elsevier 2018, pp 1-10, ISBN: 978-0-12-803581-8.

9. A.K.Matta, K.Shyam Prasad, I.Jayanth "Metal Prototyping the future of Automobile Industry: A review", elseiver, procedia material science, materials today proceedings 5(9),17597-17601,2018.

10. A.K.Matta, K.Shyam Prasad, Jayanth Chavali, Adapa Dinesh Babu, Adhitya kumar Chukka, "Computer-aided Engineering for four wheeler accelerator pedal", IJPAM, vol.18, issue 24, 2018. PP.1-10, ISSN:1314-3395.

11. A.K.Matta. How to develop a component and file a patent: More Books, ISBN: 9786202302289, 2017.

12. A.K.Matta, N.Tamiloli, P.S.Prem Kumar, S.Mohanty, S.S.Pattnaik "Experimental analysis of Erosive behavior on Al-Sicp based MMC using micro particle (Al_2O_3) as Erodent", IOP Conference Series: Material science and engineering, 455(1), , pages 012094, 2017.

13. A.K.Matta,N.Tamiloli, P.S.Prem Kumar, S.Mohanty, S.S.Pattnaik"Problems and Challenges in MMC contributing to RP ", IJMTST, vol.04, issue 1, 2017 ISSN: 2455-3778.

14. A.K.Matta, Dr.D.Ranga Raju, Dr.K.N.S.Suman "C based design Methodology and topological change for an Indian Agricultural tractor component, journal of the Institution of Engineers(India): Series A., Springer, vol.04, issue.13, pp.375-378, 2017, ISSN:2250- 2149, 2017.

15. https://rapid-prototyping-consultancy.business.site. 2017.

16. A.K.Matta, D.Ranga Raju, K.N.S.Suman (2016). An approach to predict loads on Tractor rockshaft arm. ICAI, Space society of mechanical engineers,Gujarat, ISBN 978-93-85016-99-8, 5th to 6thapril, PP.290-293.

17. A.K.Matta,"Preparation and toughness studies of Acetal (POM) & PTFE blend", vol.no.2,issue 12,IJMTST, dec 2016, ISSN:2455- 3778, pp 63- 67, 2016.

18. A.K.Matta,"Modeling of micro turbine for Rapid prototyping", vol.no.2,issue 7,IJMTST, july 2016, ISSN:2455- 3778, pp 19- 22.

19. A.K.Matta, Dr.D.RangaRaju, Dr.K.N.S.Suman "Modeling and optimization of Rapid prototyping for an Agricultural Tractor component", Discovery Engineering, 2016. vol.04, issue.13, pp.375-378, ISSN:2320- 6675.

20. A.K.Matta, Dr.D.RangaRaju, Dr.K.N.S.Suman, "3D Design support and software compensation for Rapid Virtual prototyping of Tractor Rockshaft arm", Taylor and Francis, ICCASCE-2015,Soth korea,21-22 ndAugust 2015.

21. A.K.Matta "Optimization of Brake rotor by using Taguchi method and 3D Finite Elements ",IJAER, ISSN 0973-4562 Volume 10, Number 13, pp 33175-33177 (2015).

22. A.K.Matta, A.S.Kranthi "Fabrication of a six- Legged robot with crank and slotted lever mechanism using RF communication ", IJAER, ISSN 0973-4562 Volume 10, Number 13, pp 33170-33174 (2015).

23. A.K.Matta, "Optimization of operation parameters on a Novel internally ventilated cross drilled disc brake by using Taguchi Method " IJESTA ISSN 2395-0900 Volume 1, Number 5 (2015), pp. 8-14.

24. A.K.Matta, Dr.D.RangaRaju, Dr.K.N.S.Suman, "The integration of CAD/CAM and RapidPrototyping in Product Development A review", elseiver, procedia material science pp.3438- 3445,vol.2,2015.

25. A.K.Matta,Dr.R.UmamaheswaraRao,Dr.K.N.S.Suman,Dr.V.Rambabu, "Preparation and characterization of Biodegradable PLA/PCL polymeric Blends", elseiver, procedia material science 6 (2014) pp.1266-1270.

26. Shasikumar.G.Totad, A.S.Kranti, A.K.Matta, "Sparse Social Dimension Based Collective Behavior Learning in Social Networks",Springer, ICCIDM-2014 20-21st Dec 2014.

27. A.K.Matta,V.Purushottam, "Analysis of Novel Brake Rotor using FEM", AIMTDR-2014 IIT Guwahati,12-14 thDec 2014.

28. A.K.Matta ,V.Purushottam, Dr.R.UmamaheswaraRao, "Brake Rotor Design and Finite Element Analysis" IJMER ISSN 2249-0019 Volume 4, Number 1 (2014), pp. 29-33.

29. A.K.Matta ,"Development and Impact Testing of a pultruded composite material highway guardrail" Research Journal of engineering and Technology(RJET) ISSN: 0976-2973 Volume 4, Issue 3 July-Sept.,2013, pp 132-135.

30. A.K.Matta,R.UmamaheswaraRao,V.Rambabu, "Preparation and characterization of ternary blends composed of polylactide, poly(ε-carpolactone) and MWCNT", ICEMAP-2013,23rdMay2013.

31. A.K.Matta,A.S.Kanthi "Experimental Heat Transfer And Transient State Stress Analysis Of a Brake Rotor",APM-2013,CIPET,Lucknow,1-3 March 2013,PP 17.10-17.20.

32. K.PrasadaRao, G.Anuradha,M.Anil Kumar, R.UmamaheswaraRao"The Six Sigma Approach To Reduce Specific Roll Consumption In Medium Merchant & Structural Mill"(IJREST) ISSN 2250-3676Volume 2, Issue 1 July-Sept.,2013, pp 120-129.

33. A.K.Matta ,V.Purushottam, R.UmamaheswaraRao, Dr.C.L.V.R.S.V.Prasad "Construction of a Test Bench for bike rim and Brake Rotor" IOSR Journal of engineering (IOSRJEN) ISSN: 2250-3021 Volume 2, Issue 8 (August 2012), PP 40-44, 2012.

34. A.K. Matta, R.B. Pothula and R.U. Rao "Design and Analysis of Steam Turbine Blades using FEM" International Journal of Mechanical Engineering Research. ISSN 2249-0019 Volume 2, Number 2 (2012), pp. 67-73, 2012.

35. A.K Matta, D.VenkataRao, P.RameshBabu and R. UmamaheswaraRao " Analysis of Gas Turbine blades with materials N155 and INCONEL 718"

International Journal of Advances in Science and Technology, Vol.4,No.1, pp 46-50, 2012.

36. A.K.Matta, D.VenkataRao and A.SwarnaKumari "Convective Heat Transfer Analysis of Gas Turbine Blades Using Finite Element Method",IJMER , Vol1,no.3, pp 391-397 , 2011.

37. A.K.Matta,P.RameshBabu and A.SwarnaKumari "Convective Heat Transfer Analysis of Gas Turbine Blades Using Finite Element Method",ICCMM-2011,IIT Guwahati, Guwahati, 15-16 December 2011, PP 631-636.

38. N.Rao, Dr.P.Ravi Kumar, K.S.Raghuram, M.Anil Kumar, "T24-Experimental Investigation of Neem Oil as a fuel in CI Engine" , ACME, Erode, Tamilnadu, , 25-26 March 2010, PP 626-633.

Ap Tourism: Budampadu

India's Uppalapadu Bird Sanctuary is situated there, close to Guntur City approximately 25 km from Tenali & 38 km from vijayawada. The village water tanks are used by painted storks, spot-billed pelicans, and other migratory birds from places like Siberia and Australia to build their nests.

Previously, there were roughly 12,000 birds roosting in these tanks, but recently, only about 7000 birds do so throughout the year. However, several measures have been made, such as installing artificial trees, raising local awareness, providing the ponds with enough water supply, etc. There may be more than 1500 pelicans. In addition to the six pintail ducks mentioned above, a few cormorants, five red crested pochards (rhodonesa rufina), common coots, common teal, black-headed ibises, and two stilts were also seen.

The forest department should plant more Prosopis velutina trees in and around this wetland rather than installing wire mesh artificial trees. Along with a jungle crow, the ibises and painted stork were discovered scavenging on pelican's leftover rotting fish droppings. Both fresh and salt water fish were fed to the chicks as their primary food. Some of the fish that had fallen from the nests were fresh and weighed about 0.8 kg, especially the LabeoRohita (Carp) and other sea fish. Since the pelicans were not observed fishing from adjacent ponds, they must have been transported from the nearest river and sea, which are around 20 to 30 kilometres away from the site.

Uppalapadu Bird Reserve

Despite not doing so in the first few years, in 2009 the pelicans are using the enormous wire mesh trees that the Forest department gave to build nests. In 2009, this pelicanary's ten-year run came to an end. A few pelicans have chosen to use a different pond at Ramchandrapalem, which is approximately 4 km away in the direction of Guntur.

AP Tourism: Budampadu 37.7 km from Bavani Islands